Patterson Elementary School
3731 Lawrence Drive
Naperville, IL 60564

BELUGA WHALES

by Mary Berendes

Published in the United States of America by The Child's World®
1980 Lookout Drive • Mankato, MN 56003-1705
800-599-READ • www.childsworld.com

PHOTO CREDITS

© Bryan & Cherry Alexander/Photo Researchers, Inc.: 20–21
© Chris A. Crumley/Alamy: cover, 1
© David Shale/naturepl.com: 19
© Doc White/naturepl.com: 27
© John K.B. Ford/Ursus/SeaPics.com: 13
© Kevin Schafer/Corbis: 24–25
© marinethemes.com/Kelvin Aitken: 5
© marinethemes.com/Paul Jackson: 11
© Masa Ushioda/imagequestmarine.com: 16–17
© Masa Ushioda/SeaPics.com: 6–7
© Peter Steiner/Alamy: 14–15
© Sue Flood/naturepl.com: 23
© Tami Chappell/Reuters/Corbis: 9
© Tim McGuire/Corbis: 28
© Visual & Written SL/Alamy: 10

ACKNOWLEDGMENTS

The Child's World®: Mary Berendes, Publishing Director;
Katherine Stevenson, Editor; Pamela Mitsakos, Photo Researcher;
Judy Karren, Fact Checker

The Design Lab: Kathleen Petelinsek, Design and Page Production

LIBRARY OF CONGRESS CATALOGING-IN-PUBLICATION DATA

Berendes, Mary.
  Beluga whales / by Mary Berendes.
    p. cm. — (New naturebooks)
  Includes index.
  ISBN-13: 978-1-59296-843-5 (library bound : alk. paper)
  ISBN-10: 1-59296-843-0 (library bound : alk. paper)
  1. White whale—Juvenile literature. I. Title. II. Series.
  QL737.C433B6 2007
  599.5'42—dc22   2006103442

Table of Contents

On the cover: This adult beluga whale lives at Canada's Vancouver Aquarium.

Meet the Beluga Whale!

Beluga whales are also called white whales.

The earliest beluga-whale relative lived about 10 million years ago.

In the freezing waters of the far north, huge chunks of ice float on the surface of the sea. Suddenly, a white animal rises to the surface of the water. It blows a spray of water into the air—WHOOSH! Then the creature quickly disappears. What could it be? It's a beluga (buh-LOO-guh) whale!

Beluga whales can be very curious. This one is swimming toward the photographer for a closer look.

What Are Beluga Whales?

"Beluga" comes from the Russian word *belukha*, which means "white."

The beluga's scientific name, *Delphinapterus leucas*, means "white dolphin without a wing." The "wing" would be a dorsal fin. Dolphins have a dorsal fin, but belugas don't.

Beluga whales are one of the smaller types of whales. They belong to a group known as "toothed whales." This group also includes dolphins, porpoises, narwhals, killer whales, and sperm whales. Even though toothed whales live in the water, they're not fish. They're **mammals**. Mammals are animals with warm bodies. They also feed their babies milk from their bodies. Dogs, cows, and people are mammals, too.

Beluga whales are special in many ways. Unlike other whales, they can bend their necks. Some sea mammals have a dorsal fin on their back. Belugas have only a low ridge. Without the fin, they can swim up close under floating ice.

This beluga whale lives at a zoo. The giant tank has an underwater window where visitors can watch the whale swim and play.

What Do Beluga Whales Look Like?

As beluga whales get older, their tails become more and more curved.

Beluga whales' skin is 10 times thicker than the skin of dolphins. It's the only whale skin thick enough to be used as leather.

Many belugas shed their skin each year. They rub their bodies on rocky river bottoms to get rid of the older, yellow skin.

Beluga whales are beautiful animals. Their round white bodies can bend and turn easily. Their tails are powerful. They have small, dark eyes and good eyesight—above or below the water.

Many belugas are about 10 to 15 feet (3 to 5 m) long. Some of them weigh over 3,000 pounds (1,361 kg). That's as heavy as a car! Up to half of their weight comes from a thick layer of fat called **blubber**. The blubber can be up to 4 inches (10 cm) thick. It helps keep the belugas warm.

8

These belugas live in a giant aquarium in Georgia. You can see the blubber on the belly of the lower beluga.

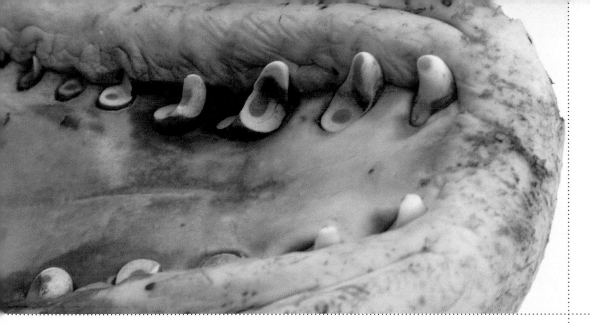

Here you can see what a beluga's teeth look like up close.

A beluga whale's head is different from that of other whales. Belugas have a large, fatty forehead called a **melon**. It changes shape when the animal makes sounds. Scientists think the melon helps with **echolocation**—that's a way of bouncing sound off things and listening to the echoes. Echolocation helps belugas find their way around and find food. The beluga's melon helps beam sound forward through the water.

Beluga whales also have a strangely shaped snout. It looks a little like a bird's beak! The beluga's snout is called a **rostrum**. Inside a beluga's mouth are about 40 peg-shaped teeth. The whale uses them to grasp slippery food.

Beluga whales have two small ear holes, one behind each eye. Scientists aren't sure if the belugas can hear through the holes. They think the whales pick up sounds through their lower jawbones instead.

This beluga is opening its mouth wide for a zookeeper. You can clearly see the whale's peg-shaped teeth.

11

Where Do Beluga Whales Live?

Only three kinds of whales live in the Artic: belugas, bowhead whales, and narwhals.

The pull of the sun and the moon causes ocean tides. The water near shore goes slowly up and down. Belugas sometimes get stuck on shore for hours when the tide gets low. They can usually stay alive until the water rises again.

Beluga whales live in cold ocean waters in and near the Arctic. They are found along the northern coasts of Alaska, Canada, Greenland, Europe, and Asia. Some live as far south as the St. Lawrence River in Canada.

Little is known about belugas' winter life. Often they swim near sea ice while looking for things to eat. But in summer, they gather in warm, shallow bays and around the outlets of rivers, called **estuaries**. Some belugas travel over 1,500 miles (2,400 km) to reach their summer homes. Some swim up into large rivers. Often they swim in very shallow water—just deep enough to cover their bodies.

The belugas' white color helps them stay alive. The white matches the snow and ice where the belugas live. Unless an enemy looks very closely, a beluga looks like a floating piece of ice.

This beluga is swimming off the coast of Canada's Northwest Territories.

How Do Beluga Whales Breathe?

Beluga whales usually dive for only 2 to 5 minutes. But they can stay underwater for as long as 15 minutes.

When a beluga breathes out, water around the blowhole sprays into the air. A beluga's "blow" can spray 3 feet (1 m) high!

Like other mammals, beluga whales need to breathe air. All whales and dolphins breathe through a **blowhole**. It's a hole on top of the animal's head. The blowhole is covered by a flap of muscle and skin. The flap keeps water out.

When a beluga swims underwater, it keeps its blowhole closed and holds its breath. When it gets near the surface, it opens the blowhole and puffs out the air. Then it takes in a quick breath and closes the flap again.

14

This young beluga's blowhole is open as it takes a breath.

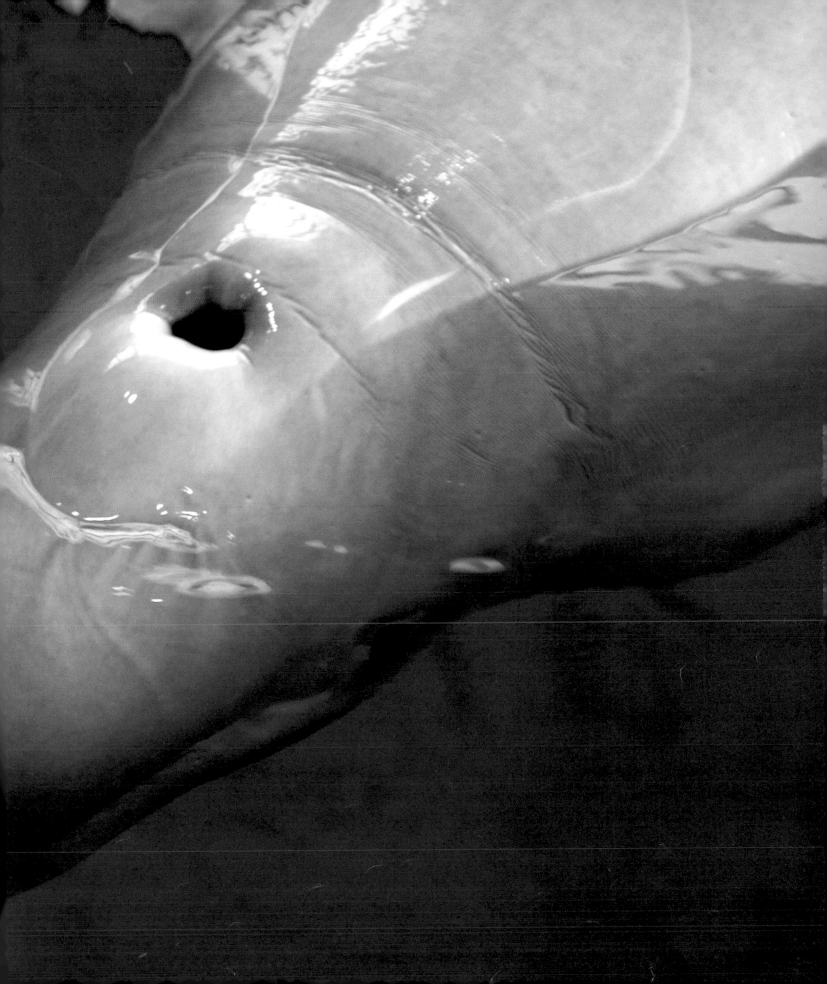

How Do Beluga Whales Swim?

Unlike most whales, belugas can swim both forward and backward.

Belugas often dive to a depth of 20 to 100 feet (about 6 to 30 m). But they've been known to dive over 2,000 feet (610 m) deep!

Beluga whales use their powerful tails to push them through the water. As the tail pumps up and down, the two end sections (called **flukes**) push the whale forward. Toward the whale's front end, two **flippers** help it change directions. The flippers look a lot like paddles. On the inside, the flippers have bones somewhat like the bones of your hand.

Beluga whales usually swim slowly—perhaps 5 miles (8 km) an hour. You could walk almost that fast! If it needs to, a beluga can swim as fast as 14 miles (23 km) an hour for a short time.

16

These two belugas live in a zoo. You can see how they pump their powerful tails to move about their tank.

What Do Beluga Whales Eat?

Belugas are "opportunistic feeders." That means they will eat almost anything, as long as it's easy to get.

Belugas don't chew their food—they swallow it whole.

Belugas sometimes work together to drive fish into shallow water. Then they scoop them up!

Beluga whales eat lots of fish such as cod, herring, and smelt. They eat squid, shrimp, and octopus as well. They also find foods such as snails, crabs, and sandworms near the ocean bottom.

Beluga whales sometimes end up being food for other animals, too! Belugas need to be especially careful when they are feeding. That's because killer whales sometimes sneak up and attack them. When belugas come up for air—or if they get trapped by ice—hungry polar bears might be waiting for them. To stay safe, belugas need to be careful all the time.

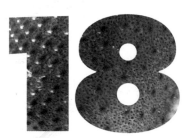

Squid might look funny, but belugas find them to be a tasty treat!

Do Beluga Whales Stay Together?

Beluga pods are usually made up of whales of about the same age. Pods often have two to 25 whales.

Sometimes small pods come together to form larger pods, especially when the animals travel. Sometimes pods have hundreds or even thousands of belugas.

Belugas switch pods often, sometimes from week to week.

Beluga whales tend to live in groups called **pods**. The whales of a pod eat, play, and travel together. They also protect each other from enemies. Most pods have males and females and are led by a large male. But some pods include only mothers and babies, or only males. Babies learn how to find food and stay safe by watching the pod's older whales.

Many animals like to be alone—but not belugas! They often rub up against each other or touch their flippers. Scientists think touching helps the whales "talk" to each other. By touching and rubbing, they might be saying "Here I am!" or "Let's play!"

This pod of belugas is swimming in Hudson Bay, Canada. They are near the mouth of the Seal River.

What Are Baby Belugas Like?

Beluga females usually give birth to a single calf every three years.

Baby belugas are gray. They get lighter as they grow older. They are white by the time they're adults—when they're about five to seven years old.

After male and female belugas mate, a baby starts to grow inside the female's body. The baby grows for a little over a year before it is ready to be born. The females usually have their babies, or **calves**, in the warm waters around estuaries. Depending on where the mothers live, the calves are born sometime between March and September. Most of them are born in May through July.

When the calf is born, it is already 5 feet (about a meter and a half) long and weighs about 175 pounds (79 kg). It can swim right away. Beluga calves drink only their mother's milk for a whole year, until their teeth grow in. They then start eating small fish and shrimp. But they keep drinking their mothers' milk for up to two years.

This young calf is swimming with its mother off the coast of Canada.

What Sounds Do Beluga Whales Make?

Even when the water is covered with ice, belugas can find holes for breathing. Scientists think the belugas use echolocation to find these open areas.

Scientists have recorded dozens of different beluga whale sounds.

Beluga whales' sounds can sometimes be heard by people on shore or even inside ships.

Beluga whales make lots of noises. They make clicking sounds for echolocation. Their melon beams the clicks through the water. The sounds bounce off objects and return as echoes. The echoes tell the whale where the objects are, what sizes and shapes they are, and even how fast they're moving. The whale can use echolocation to find food, the sea bottom, and ice at the surface.

Belugas make many other sounds, too. In fact, they are sometimes called "sea canaries" because they sound like underwater birds! The belugas use these sounds to talk to each other while they are swimming.

24

This beluga is communicating with its pod as the whales swim in Hudson Bay near Manitoba, Canada.

Are Beluga Whales in Danger?

Belugas' living places have been changed by people bringing in ships, building dams, making other changes along rivers and bays, and drilling for oil.

The St. Lawrence River is very dirty. Belugas that live there are full of pollutants. When they die, their bodies are handled as "toxic waste"—garbage that is poisonous.

Today, many beluga populations are in danger. For thousands of years, Native peoples in the Arctic hunted belugas. They needed the animals' meat, blubber, and skin. Then other people started killing many more belugas to sell the meat, oil, and skin. The oil in the beluga's melons was thought to be especially fine. From the 1700s into the 1900s, tens of thousands of belugas were killed. The whales faced other dangers, too. More people started building and living along coastlines and rivers where the whales live. The water became **polluted**.

Today, no one knows exactly how many belugas are left—perhaps 62,000 to 80,000. Especially in some areas, there are far fewer than there used to be. Some local groups of belugas are in danger of dying out completely.

26

This whale is raising its head above the water to check out its surroundings. It's swimming with about twenty other whales off Canada's coast.

Scientists are trying to learn more about beluga whales. They are trying to figure out what the whales' sounds mean. They are studying how and where belugas live at different times of the year. They are learning how different groups of belugas are related. And they are studying the effects of water pollution and building along shorelines.

Belugas are an important part of their ocean world. Their health tells us a lot about the condition of the waters in which they live. Many people are working to figure out how to balance the needs of beluga whales and people. They are hoping that we can have healthy belugas swimming free in their northern waters far into the future.

Some Arctic peoples still hunt belugas for food. Belugas are an important part of these peoples' way of life.

Beluga whales can live for 30 years or perhaps longer.

Many zoos have beluga whales that people can see.

Aquariums are great places to see beluga whales up close!

29

Glossary

blowhole (BLOH-hole) A blowhole is a breathing hole in the top of a sea mammal's head. Whales and dolphins breathe through a blowhole.

blubber (BLUH-ber) Blubber is a layer of fat under the skin of sea mammals that helps the animals stay warm. Beluga whales have a thick layer of blubber.

calves (KAVZ) Calves are the young of some kinds of animals, such as cows, elephants, or whales. Beluga whale calves can swim when they are born.

echolocation (eh-ko-lo-KAY-shun) Echolocation is a way in which some animals use sound to "see" what is around them. They find and identify nearby objects by sending out sounds and listing to the echoes. Beluga whales use echolocation.

estuaries (ESS-choo-wer-eez) Estuaries are wide areas of water where rivers flow into the sea. Belugas live in and around estuaries during the summer.

flippers (FLIH-purz) Flippers are the broad, flat legs of some sea animals that act like paddles to help the animals swim. A beluga whale has two flippers towards its front end.

flukes (FLOOKS) Flukes are the flat, triangular parts on the sides of a whale's tail. Beluga whales' flukes push the whales through the water.

mammals (MAM-ullz) Mammals are warm-blooded animals that usually have hair on their bodies and that feed their babies milk from the mother's body. Adult belugas don't have hair, but they're still mammals.

melon (MEL-un) A melon is the big, rounded part on the heads of some sea mammals. A beluga whale's melon helps the animal send out sounds for echolocation.

pods (PODZ) Groups of some types of animals are called pods. Beluga whales live and travel in pods.

polluted (puh-LOO-tud) Something that is polluted is dirty. Heavier use of coastlines has polluted many areas where belugas live.

rostrum (ROS-trum) The beaklike snout of some animals is called a rostrum. Beluga whales have a rostrum.

To Find Out More

Read It!

Gunzi, Christiane. *The Best Book of Whales and Dolphins.* New York: Kingfisher, 2001.

Hirschmann, Kris. *Beluga Whales.* San Diego: Kidhaven Press, 2004.

Johnston, Marianne. *Beluga Whales and Their Babies.* New York: PowerKids Press, 1999.

Lingemann, Linda, and Jon Weiman (illustrator). *Beluga Passage.* Norwalk, CT: Soundprints, 1996.

Sayre, April Pulley. *Secrets of Sound: Studying the Calls and Songs of Whales, Elephants, and Birds.* Boston: Houghton Mifflin, 2002.

Schuch, Steve, and Peter Sylvada (illustrator). *A Symphony of Whales.* San Diego: Voyager Books, 1999.

On the Web

Visit our Web page for lots of links about beluga whales:
http://www.childsworld.com/links

Note to Parents, Teachers, and Librarians: We routinely check our Web links to make sure they're safe, active sites—so encourage your readers to check them out!

31

Index

About the Author

Mary Berendes has loved books and writing for as long as she can remember. An author of over twenty children's books, Mary especially enjoys writing about nature and animals. Mary has long been a collector of antique books, and owns several that are almost two hundred years old. She lives in Minnesota.